Our Daily Bread

Prayer Journal

With Writing Prompts

Prayer is asking for rain. Faith is bringing an umbrella

Copyright © 2019 Ubora Press

All rights reserved.

This journal belongs to...

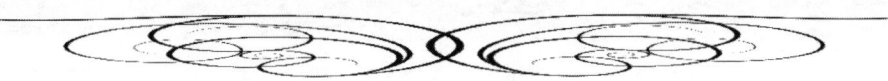

Month_____   Year_____

Sunday	Monday	Tuesday	Wednesday	Thursday	Friday	Saturday

Notes

I Give Thanks For

Date

People I Will Pray For

Personal Challenges

Society And Government

Don't be afraid, just Believe — Mark 5:36

Reflections

I Give Thanks For

Date

People I Will Pray For

Personal Challenges

Society And Government

Always Believe, Have Faith & Pray

Reflections

I Give Thanks For

Date

Personal Challenges

People I Will Pray For

Society And Government

> And we know that in all things God works for the good of those who love him, who have been called according to his purpose.

Reflections

I Give Thanks For

Date

People I Will Pray For

Personal Challenges

Society And Government

A.S.A.P.
always say a prayer

Reflections

I Give Thanks For

Date

People I Will Pray For

Personal Challenges

Society And Government

Be on your Guard
Stand firm in the faith.
Be courageous be strong
Do everything in love.

Reflections

I Give Thanks For

Date

People I Will Pray For

Personal Challenges

Society And Government

Believe

Reflections

I Give Thanks For

Date

People I Will Pray For

Personal Challenges

Society And Government

Child Of God

Reflections

I Give Thanks For

Date

People I Will Pray For

Personal Challenges

Society And Government

Child of the One True King

Reflections

I Give Thanks For

Date

People I Will Pray For

Personal Challenges

Society And Government

COUNT YOUR
BLESSINGS
𝍫 ||

Reflections

I Give Thanks For

Date

People I Will Pray For

Personal Challenges

Society And Government

Do not JUDGE

Reflections

I Give Thanks For

Date

People I Will Pray For

Personal Challenges

Society And Government

Do to others as you would have them do to you

Reflections

I Give Thanks For

Date

People I Will Pray For

Personal Challenges

Society And Government

Don't BE AFRAID, JUST Believe — MARK 5:36

Reflections

I Give Thanks For

Date

People I Will Pray For

Personal Challenges

Society And Government

DON'T JUDGE SOMEONE
JUST BECAUSE THEY SIN
differently THAN YOU

Reflections

I Give Thanks For

Date

People I Will Pray For

Personal Challenges

Society And Government

Faith Can Move Mountains

Reflections

I Give Thanks For

Date

People I Will Pray For

Personal Challenges

Society And Government

Faith Is Seeing Light With Your Heart When All Your Eyes See Is Darkness

Reflections

I Give Thanks For

_____
_____

_____
_____

Date

_____

People I Will Pray For

_____
_____
_____
_____
_____
_____
_____
_____
_____

Personal Challenges

_____
_____
_____
_____
_____

Society And Government

_____
_____
_____
_____

Faith Over Fear

Reflections

_____
_____
_____
_____

I Give Thanks For

_____
_____
_____
_____

Personal Challenges

_____
_____
_____
_____
_____

Society And Government

_____
_____
_____
_____

Date

_____

People I Will Pray For

_____
_____
_____
_____
_____
_____
_____
_____

Faith WILL GET YOU Everywhere

Reflections

_____
_____
_____
_____

I Give Thanks For

Date

People I Will Pray For

Personal Challenges

Society And Government

Faith

Reflections

I Give Thanks For

Date

People I Will Pray For

Personal Challenges

Society And Government

I AM FEARFULLY AND WONDERFULLY made
PSALM 139:14

Reflections

I Give Thanks For

Date

People I Will Pray For

Personal Challenges

Society And Government

Follow MY EXAMPLE, AS I FOLLOW the example of *Christ*.
— I CORINTHIANS 11:1 —

Reflections

I Give Thanks For

_____
_____
_____
_____

Personal Challenges

_____
_____
_____
_____
_____

Society And Government

_____
_____
_____
_____

Reflections

_____
_____
_____
_____

Date

_____

People I Will Pray For

_____
_____
_____
_____
_____
_____
_____
_____
_____

FOR THIS Child I HAVE prayed
—1 Samuel 1:27—

I Give Thanks For

_____
_____
_____
_____

Personal Challenges

_____
_____
_____
_____
_____

Society And Government

_____
_____
_____
_____

Date

_____

People I Will Pray For

_____
_____
_____
_____
_____
_____
_____
_____

Gather here with grateful hearts

Reflections

_____
_____
_____
_____

I Give Thanks For

Date

People I Will Pray For

Personal Challenges

Society And Government

God brings you to it
He will bring you through it

Reflections

I Give Thanks For

Date

People I Will Pray For

Personal Challenges

Society And Government

God is Good

Reflections

I Give Thanks For

Date

People I Will Pray For

Personal Challenges

Society And Government

> God is Preparing you for something great. Just hold on.

Reflections

I Give Thanks For

_____
_____
_____
_____

Personal Challenges

_____
_____
_____
_____
_____

Society And Government

_____
_____
_____
_____

Date

_____

People I Will Pray For

_____
_____
_____
_____
_____
_____
_____
_____
_____
_____

Grateful & Blessed

Reflections

_____
_____
_____
_____

I Give Thanks For

Date

People I Will Pray For

Personal Challenges

Society And Government

Handle with prayer

Reflections

I Give Thanks For

Date

People I Will Pray For

Personal Challenges

Society And Government

>> HAVE <<
patience.
> GOD <
ISN'T FINISHED YET
PHILIPPIANS 1:6

Reflections

I Give Thanks For

Date

People I Will Pray For

Personal Challenges

Society And Government

> I AM THE *Vine*,
> YOU ARE THE BRANCHES.
> APART FROM ME YOU CAN DO *Nothing*
> JOHN 15:5

Reflections

I Give Thanks For

Date

People I Will Pray For

Personal Challenges

Society And Government

I am a child of God

Reflections

I Give Thanks For

_____
_____
_____
_____

Personal Challenges

_____
_____
_____
_____
_____

Society And Government

_____
_____
_____
_____

Reflections

_____
_____
_____
_____
_____

Date

_____

People I Will Pray For

_____
_____
_____
_____
_____
_____
_____
_____
_____
_____

— I CAN DO —
ALL THINGS
through Christ
✦ *which* ✦
STRENGTHEN
— ME —

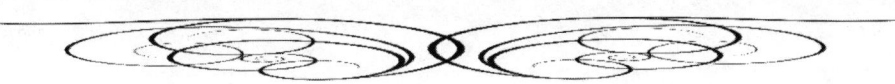

Month_____ Year_____

Sunday	Monday	Tuesday	Wednesday	Thursday	Friday	Saturday

Notes

Month_____ Year_____

Sunday	Monday	Tuesday	Wednesday	Thursday	Friday	Satturday

Notes

I Give Thanks For

Date

People I Will Pray For

Personal Challenges

Society And Government

IF THE SON Sets you FREE YOU will be FREE indeed — John 8:36

Reflections

I Give Thanks For

Date

People I Will Pray For

Personal Challenges

Society And Government

In all things GOD WORKS FOR THE GOOD OF THOSE — WHO — LOVE HIM

Reflections

I Give Thanks For

Date

People I Will Pray For

Personal Challenges

Society And Government

Love is patient
LOVE IS KIND.
It does not envy,
IT DOES NOT BOAST,
it is not proud
1 CORINTHIANS 13:4

Reflections

I Give Thanks For

Date

People I Will Pray For

Personal Challenges

Society And Government

Love Pray and Be Thankful

Reflections

I Give Thanks For

Date

People I Will Pray For

Personal Challenges

Society And Government

Not Today Satan

Reflections

I Give Thanks For

Date

People I Will Pray For

Personal Challenges

Society And Government

Prayers go up
Blessings go down

Reflections

I Give Thanks For

Date

Personal Challenges

People I Will Pray For

Society And Government

Simply Blessed

Reflections

I Give Thanks For

_____
_____
_____
_____

Personal Challenges

_____
_____
_____
_____
_____

Society And Government

_____
_____
_____
_____
_____

Date

_____

People I Will Pray For

_____
_____
_____
_____
_____
_____
_____
_____
_____

The Lord
IS MY GUIDE

Reflections

_____
_____
_____
_____
_____

I Give Thanks For

Date

People I Will Pray For

Personal Challenges

Society And Government

> Trust in
> the Lord
> with all your heart

Reflections

I Give Thanks For

Date

People I Will Pray For

Personal Challenges

Society And Government

WE WALK BY FAITH NOT BY SIGHT

Reflections

I Give Thanks For

Date

People I Will Pray For

Personal Challenges

Society And Government

What God
KNOWS ABOUT ME
IS MORE IMPORTANT
than what others
THINK ABOUT ME

Reflections

I Give Thanks For

Date

People I Will Pray For

Personal Challenges

Society And Government

WHEN LIFE GETS
TOO HARD TO STAND
Kneel

Reflections

I Give Thanks For

Date

People I Will Pray For

Personal Challenges

Society And Government

YOUR FAITH CAN MOVE THE MOUNTAINS THAT YOUR DOUBT IN HIM Has Created

Reflections

I Give Thanks For

Date

People I Will Pray For

Personal Challenges

Society And Government

Always Believe, Have Faith & Pray

Reflections

I Give Thanks For

Date

People I Will Pray For

Personal Challenges

Society And Government

And we know that in all things God works for the good of those who love him, who have been called according to his purpose.

Reflections

I Give Thanks For

Date

People I Will Pray For

Personal Challenges

Society And Government

A.S.A.P.
always say a prayer

Reflections

I Give Thanks For

Date

People I Will Pray For

Personal Challenges

Society And Government

Be on your Guard
Stand firm in the faith.
Be courageous be strong
Do everything in love.

Reflections

I Give Thanks For

_____
_____
_____
_____

Personal Challenges

_____
_____
_____
_____

Society And Government

_____
_____
_____
_____

Reflections

_____
_____
_____
_____

Date

_____

People I Will Pray For

_____
_____
_____
_____
_____
_____
_____
_____

Believe

I Give Thanks For

Date

People I Will Pray For

Personal Challenges

Society And Government

Reflections

I Give Thanks For

Date

People I Will Pray For

Personal Challenges

Society And Government

Child of the One True King

Reflections

I Give Thanks For

Date

People I Will Pray For

Personal Challenges

Society And Government

COUNT YOUR BLESSINGS
✝✝✝✝✝ ✝✝

Reflections

I Give Thanks For

Date

People I Will Pray For

Personal Challenges

Society And Government

Do not JUDGE

Reflections

I Give Thanks For

Date

People I Will Pray For

Personal Challenges

Society And Government

Do to others as you would have them do to you

Reflections

I Give Thanks For

Date

People I Will Pray For

Personal Challenges

Society And Government

Don't be afraid, just Believe — Mark 5:36

Reflections

I Give Thanks For

Date

Personal Challenges

People I Will Pray For

Society And Government

DON'T JUDGE SOMEONE
JUST BECAUSE THEY SIN
differently THAN YOU

Reflections

I Give Thanks For

Date

People I Will Pray For

Personal Challenges

Society And Government

Faith Can Move Mountains

Reflections

I Give Thanks For

Date

People I Will Pray For

Personal Challenges

Society And Government

Faith Is Seeing Light With Your Heart When All Your Eyes SEE Is Darkness

Reflections

I Give Thanks For

Date

People I Will Pray For

Personal Challenges

Society And Government

Faith Over Fear

Reflections

I Give Thanks For

Date

Personal Challenges

People I Will Pray For

Society And Government

Faith WILL GET YOU Everywhere

Reflections

I Give Thanks For

Date

People I Will Pray For

Personal Challenges

Society And Government

Gather here with grateful hearts

Reflections

I Give Thanks For

Date

People I Will Pray For

Personal Challenges

Society And Government

God brings you to it
He will bring you through it

Reflections

*Month*_____ *Year*_____

Sunday	Monday	Tuesday	Wednesday	Thursday	Friday	Satturday

Notes

I Give Thanks For

Date

People I Will Pray For

Personal Challenges

Society And Government

FOR THIS
Child
I HAVE
prayed
— 1 Samuel 1:27 —

Reflections

I Give Thanks For

_____
_____
_____
_____

Date

_____

People I Will Pray For

_____
_____
_____
_____
_____
_____
_____
_____

Personal Challenges

_____
_____
_____
_____

Society And Government

_____
_____
_____
_____

Gather here with grateful hearts

Reflections

_____
_____
_____
_____
_____

I Give Thanks For

Date

People I Will Pray For

Personal Challenges

Society And Government

God brings you to it
He will bring you through it

Reflections

I Give Thanks For

Date

People I Will Pray For

Personal Challenges

Society And Government

God is Good

Reflections

I Give Thanks For

Date

Personal Challenges

People I Will Pray For

Society And Government

> God is Preparing you for something great. Just hold on.

Reflections

I Give Thanks For

_____
_____
_____
_____

Date

_____

People I Will Pray For

_____
_____
_____
_____
_____
_____
_____
_____
_____

Personal Challenges

_____
_____
_____
_____
_____

Society And Government

_____
_____
_____
_____

Grateful & Blessed

Reflections

_____
_____
_____
_____
_____

I Give Thanks For

Date

People I Will Pray For

Personal Challenges

Society And Government

Handle with prayer

Reflections

I Give Thanks For

Date

People I Will Pray For

Personal Challenges

Society And Government

→→ HAVE ←←
patience.
GOD
ISN'T FINISHED YET
PHILIPPIANS 1:6

Reflections

I Give Thanks For

Date

People I Will Pray For

Personal Challenges

Society And Government

HE KNOWS THE WAY
BECAUSE
He IS THE *way*

Reflections

I Give Thanks For
_____
_____
_____
_____

Date
_____

People I Will Pray For
_____
_____
_____
_____
_____
_____
_____
_____

Personal Challenges
_____
_____
_____
_____

Society And Government
_____
_____
_____
_____

I am a child of God

Reflections
_____
_____
_____
_____

I Give Thanks For

Date

Personal Challenges

People I Will Pray For

Society And Government

I AM THE *Vine,*
YOU ARE THE BRANCHES.
APART FROM ME YOU CAN DO *Nothing*
JOHN 15:5

Reflections

I Give Thanks For

Date

People I Will Pray For

Personal Challenges

Society And Government

> — I CAN DO —
> ALL THINGS
> *through Christ*
> *which*
> STRENGTHEN
> — ME —

Reflections

I Give Thanks For

Date

People I Will Pray For

Personal Challenges

Society And Government

If any of you lack wisdom let him ask GOD

Reflections

I Give Thanks For

Date

People I Will Pray For

Personal Challenges

Society And Government

IF THE SON Sets you FREE YOU will be FREE indeed — John 8:36

Reflections

I Give Thanks For

Date

People I Will Pray For

Personal Challenges

Society And Government

In all things GOD WORKS FOR THE GOOD OF THOSE — WHO — LOVE HIM

Reflections

I Give Thanks For

_____
_____
_____
_____

Personal Challenges

_____
_____
_____
_____

Society And Government

_____
_____
_____
_____

Reflections

_____
_____
_____
_____

Date

_____

People I Will Pray For

_____
_____
_____
_____
_____
_____
_____
_____

Love is patient
LOVE IS KIND.
It does not envy,
IT DOES NOT BOAST,
it is not proud

1 CORINTHIANS 13:4

I Give Thanks For

Date

People I Will Pray For

Personal Challenges

Society And Government

Love Pray and Be Thankful

Reflections

I Give Thanks For

_____
_____
_____
_____

Personal Challenges

_____
_____
_____
_____
_____

Society And Government

_____
_____
_____
_____

Reflections

_____
_____
_____
_____
_____

Date

_____

People I Will Pray For

_____
_____
_____
_____
_____
_____
_____
_____
_____
_____

Not Today Satan

I Give Thanks For

Date

People I Will Pray For

Personal Challenges

Society And Government

Prayers go up
Blessings go down

Reflections

I Give Thanks For

_____
_____
_____
_____

Date

_____

People I Will Pray For

_____
_____
_____
_____
_____
_____
_____
_____

Personal Challenges

_____
_____
_____
_____

Society And Government

_____
_____
_____
_____

Simply Blessed

Reflections

_____
_____
_____
_____

I Give Thanks For

Date

People I Will Pray For

Personal Challenges

Society And Government

The Lord
IS MY GUIDE

Reflections

I Give Thanks For

Date

People I Will Pray For

Personal Challenges

Society And Government

Trust in the Lord with all your heart

Reflections

I Give Thanks For

Date

People I Will Pray For

Personal Challenges

Society And Government

WE WALK BY FAITH NOT BY SIGHT

Reflections

I Give Thanks For

Date

People I Will Pray For

Personal Challenges

Society And Government

What God
KNOWS ABOUT ME
IS MORE IMPORTANT
than what others
THINK ABOUT ME

Reflections

I Give Thanks For

Date

People I Will Pray For

Personal Challenges

Society And Government

WHEN LIFE GETS TOO HARD TO STAND
Kneel

Reflections

I Give Thanks For

Date

People I Will Pray For

Personal Challenges

Society And Government

Always Believe, Have Faith & Pray

Reflections

I Give Thanks For

Date

People I Will Pray For

Personal Challenges

Society And Government

Love is patient
LOVE IS KIND.
It does not envy,
IT DOES NOT BOAST,
it is not proud
I CORINTHIANS 13:4

Reflections

I Give Thanks For

_____
_____
_____
_____

Personal Challenges

_____
_____
_____
_____

Society And Government

_____
_____
_____
_____

Date

_____

People I Will Pray For

_____
_____
_____
_____
_____
_____
_____
_____

Faith

Reflections

_____
_____
_____
_____

I Give Thanks For

_____
_____
_____
_____
_____

Personal Challenges

_____
_____
_____
_____
_____

Society And Government

_____
_____
_____
_____

Reflections

_____
_____
_____
_____

Date

_____

People I Will Pray For

_____
_____
_____
_____
_____
_____
_____
_____
_____
_____

Don't BE AFRAID, JUST Believe — Mark 5:36

I Give Thanks For

_____
_____
_____
_____

Personal Challenges

_____
_____
_____
_____

Society And Government

_____
_____
_____
_____

Date

_____

People I Will Pray For

_____
_____
_____
_____
_____
_____
_____
_____

COUNT YOUR BLESSINGS
𝍷𝍷𝍷𝍷𝍷 𝍷𝍷

Reflections

_____
_____
_____
_____

I Give Thanks For

Date

People I Will Pray For

Personal Challenges

Society And Government

Don't BE AFRAID, JUST Believe — Mark 5:36

Reflections

I Give Thanks For

_____
_____
_____
_____
_____

Personal Challenges

_____
_____
_____
_____
_____

Society And Government

_____
_____
_____
_____
_____

Reflections

_____
_____
_____
_____

Date

_____

People I Will Pray For

_____
_____
_____
_____
_____
_____
_____
_____
_____

A.S.A.P.
always say a prayer